T0193468

Two Hearts
One Soul

My Journey through Past Lives

JANET HOFFMAN CENZANO

iUniverse, Inc.
Bloomington

TWO HEARTS, ONE SOUL
MY JOURNEY THROUGH PAST LIVES

iUniverse books may be ordered through booksellers or by contacting:

iUniverse
1663 Liberty Drive
Bloomington, IN 47403
www.iuniverse.com
1-800-Authors (1-800-288-4677)

Because of the dynamic nature of the Internet, any web addresses or links contained in this book may have changed since publication and may no longer be valid. The views expressed in this work are solely those of the author and do not necessarily reflect the views of the publisher, and the publisher hereby disclaims any responsibility for them.

Any people depicted in stock imagery provided by Thinkstock are models, and such images are being used for illustrative purposes only.

Certain stock imagery © Thinkstock.

ISBN: 978-1-4759-7479-9 (sc)
ISBN: 978-1-4759-7480-5 (e)

Library of Congress Control Number: 2013901971

Printed in the United States of America

iUniverse rev. date: 2/14/2013

Table of Contents

Acknowledgments ix

Introduction xi

Young Love: A Story of Connection 1

Atlantic City: A Fun Time 6

New Beginnings: A Change in a Relationship 10

Henry: True Love 14

Transition: Learning to Live Alone 21

Past Lives: Tapping into My Psychic Abilities 32

Donnie: Reconnecting with My Soul Mate 42

Intuition: Everyone Has It 46

References 53

Everything really does happen for a reason,
and even if you can't understand it all,
everything that happens to you is meant to
happen for the progression of *your soul*.*

Beyond the Veil Where the Angels Ascend

*quote posted on <u>www.facebook.com/Beyondtheveil1111</u>

Acknowledgments

This book is based on a true story. The names of some people have been changed to protect their privacy.

I would like to thank all of you who have encouraged me to write this book—most of all, my son, Todd; his wife, Jen; my granddaughter, Cassie; and Aunt Betty. In addition, I would like to thank my mentors, Sue, Elaine, Al, Lourdes, and Pat, and especially Shelly, who is not only a mentor, but also a good friend.

Introduction

My story begins many lifetimes ago. I have lived five past lives, and three of them were centered on a young man who has also been a part of my present life since I was a teenager. How do I know this? It has taken me forty-some years to get to this point and finally put this puzzle together. It has been an interesting and instructive journey, and one that I would like to share with you. Throughout my experiences, you'll see how I accessed these past life memories and understand how they intertwine with this present life. I believe that most of you have had past life experiences as well and will be able to relate to my story.

I am a firm believer in karma and destiny. A coincidence, a chance, or an accidental happening can occur sometimes, but mostly it's not simply chance, especially if it happens over and over. Growing up, I repeatedly experienced the same déjà vu moments and visions of other places and people; mostly, I didn't pay too much attention to them then. But over the years, I realized these déjà vu moments were trying to tell me something specific about my past, and for this reason I began using past life regression therapy (PLR) to access more information. Through PLR, I went back to a previous lifetime through my hearing, feelings, images, thoughts, and visions. Sometimes, regression can be a vague sensation (e.g., déjà vu) that creates a sense of familiarity. Other times, it can be vivid flashes of memories of other places that you know are not a part of your present life.

In addition to PLR, however, people can remember their past lives in many other ways, including dreams, relaxation, or experiencing visions. Meditation will relax you enough to put you in an alpha state (relaxation). After this state, you will reach a theta state (drowsiness). This is the state where past memories and psychic thoughts will appear. When using meditation to access your past lives, you should be comfortable and take deep breaths and be completely relaxed in your body and your mind in order to go into your subconscious. For me, sometimes the regression is like a slide show, where I am seeing images and receiving thoughts and feelings. Other times, it is like a video, and I can stop, pausing at different frames and focusing on important matters. Using meditation to clarify past life issues has been very successful for me.

Another method I have used to access my past lives is acupuncture, which is an ancient form of Chinese healing that stimulates the pressure points in the body through the use of thin needles. This method is believed to adjust the energy flow into healthier patterns and to stimulate areas of the brain, allowing memories of past lives to surface.

These are a few avenues to try, if you choose. Let me tell you, I did it all and was quite successful. I was also fortunate enough to have a friend who is a gifted psychic medium help me. Through a past life reading, she relayed information that focused on the important issues of my past lives, including many fears about loss, solitude, separation, closed places, and women not being liberated. What I learned from working with her has amazed me—so many unexplained events in my life now make sense. For example, in high school, I was a member of the Latin club and had the chance to visit Europe. However, the thought of being in Europe scared me; I felt anxious about my safety there. These reactions always puzzled me, but my fear ran deep. After working with my friend and discovering information about my past lives, I understand now why I am so fearful about traveling to Europe. It might be to your advantage to seek a reputable psychic medium, as I did, to help you put the pieces of information together in order to access and understand your own past lives.

I don't think I have uncovered all of my past lives. I know they are stored in my subconscious and that if something is not resolved from a past life, it could resurface at anytime and be resolved in this life.

I hope my story will lift you up, motivate you, and give you a sense of hope. Never give up on yourself. When you are motivated and you want to do something, do it! Taking that first step—no matter how scary it might be—can change your life for the better, as it did mine. You will be able to see your life clearly and decide what direction to follow. Trust your intuitive feelings and see the positive changes that occur in your life.

Young Love: A Story of Connection

S ummer had ended and another school year was beginning. It was 1962, and I had just turned sixteen in July and was entering my junior year. My friends and I were looking forward to attending school games, dances, and special events. This was a special semester for me, as I was enrolled in the driver's education class. I already had my driving permit since July and was fairly good at driving a car with an adult, but I was anxious to drive and be able to go places by myself. When I arrived at the driver's ed class, I met my teacher and the four other students. All of us were anxious to get our licenses, and I knew it would be a good class because everyone got along well.

After a few classes, one of the boys, Donnie, started talking with me. He was about six feet tall, thin, and blond with blue eyes. He was very nice and not as shy as I was, and he did most of the talking at first. He made me feel comfortable, and I knew he felt the same with me. We really didn't know each other because we lived on different ends of the town and went to different elementary and junior high schools, but all the schools in the district merged for high school.

Don and I talked about our other classes and realized we were both in the third period chorus. Third period! That was too early to be singing. At tryouts for chorus, the director decided that I was a second soprano, but that I could reach some of the first soprano notes. Don told me that he was a baritone. He never told me, though, that he sang solos and was singing on a local television show every Friday night. The first time I heard him sing in chorus, his clear, rich voice gave me goose bumps up and down my arms. His voice was familiar to me. Had I ever heard him before? I just stood very still and tried to digest my feelings and thoughts.

Donnie and I became fast, close friends. When we were in the backseat of the driver's ed car observing the other student driver, we had a chance to talk and get to know each other.

As we were talking about our families, I told him that my mom, a dietician at a local middle school, was the best cook ever. He asked me if she cooked Italian food, as it was his favorite. I said of course she did—she's Italian. When I arrived home from school that day, I asked my parents if I could invite Donnie for dinner. My mom asked me questions about him and then said I could invite him for dinner the following week. He could ride home with me on the school bus, and my parents would drive him home. I felt good about him coming onto my turf instead of the other way around.

Don came over for dinner the next week. My mom made a terrific Italian dinner consisting of spaghetti, meatballs, sausage, antipasto, Italian bread, and homemade apple pie. He must have enjoyed the meal because he had two helpings of everything. He stayed awhile, and my parents had the chance to get to know him, too. As an only child,

I was close to my parents. They were good-hearted and welcoming people, and it was important to me that they liked Donnie. That evening, as my mom told stories about my childhood and my dad shared information about his work as an accountant, I was delighted that Donnie seemed to fit in so well with my family. Around 9:00 p.m., my mom and I drove him home, and he thanked her for the delicious dinner.

The next day, after class, he told me how much he enjoyed the meal and thanked me for inviting him. He chuckled and asked if he would ever be invited again. He also said that he felt comfortable with my family and that they reminded him of his.

During this semester, Donnie and I started dating. He gave me his jade ring to wear on a chain, so we were officially "going steady." From this point on we did everything and went everywhere together. For me, it felt right being together—like we fit.

Donnie and I discussed our futures, and I knew he would inevitably choose a career in singing. That was his first love, and I fully supported him. He got gigs at local nightclubs and was becoming a well-known singer/entertainer in upstate New York. He also appeared in local plays and made a name for himself as an actor. My family and I attended his plays, and I always went to the nightclub he was appearing at on Saturday nights. Our parents often went, too. We all enjoyed listening to him.

Because I was conscious of what I looked like, I wore a pretty dress with heels and my long, curly hair up in a French twist. I wanted to look nice for him and for the people we met there. Every time I attended, I sat at the table facing Don. I knew his last song was for me. Afterward, he and I would go to the diner for breakfast.

As time went on, our families became friends, and we frequently had get-togethers. It seemed like we had known each other for a long time, and it was a comfortable relationship for all. We especially liked Donnie's sister, Joy, and her husband, Chuck. During one of our outings, his family told us that they had come from the Netherlands in 1948 and settled in this area because they had family here. Sometimes, when they were talking about their homeland, I would get quick flashes of images relating to what they were saying, such as an image of flat land with hills. I immediately dismissed it as just a fluke, thinking perhaps I had seen a photo or picture of Holland's countryside.

Don often told me I could easily blend in as a Dutch girl, even though I was Italian and German. With my fair coloring, I guess I could. The first time he said this, I had a flash of me in Holland as a young girl wearing a hat, a dress, and wooden shoes, and kneeling by rows of tulips. It felt so real. *How weird,* I thought. I didn't know anything about Holland! Or did I?

In January 1963, during the second semester of school, Don and I decided to take a personal typing class. We managed to get seats next to one another, and it was fun. He would always comment on how much faster I could type than he could. We both got a chuckle out of that. Before the semester began, we would check out where our classes were located and when and where we could meet up. Because there wasn't much time between classes and we couldn't talk, we would write notes to each other and make after-school plans. He always called me, though, at least once when he arrived home from school. Our big day came in February when we both took our driver's test in icy, snowy weather. Luckily, we both passed. Hooray!

Around that time, Donnie acquired an agent in New York City who was helping him build his singing career. We skipped school a couple of times to drive to New York City so he could meet with her. (By the way, our parents were aware of us not going to school—we were trustworthy teens!) Other times, we went to the city on our school breaks or days off. My parents were nice enough to let us use their car. Sometimes, they even came with us. We all had fun during those trips, walking the New York City streets, shopping, and going to dinner. We packed in a lot for one day. One time we couldn't drive home because we got caught in an unexpected snowstorm and the Thruway was closed. We just made the best of it, stayed over, and drove home the next day.

Atlantic City: A Fun Time

B y summer, Donnie and I were spending a lot of time together, especially now that we were both driving. If Don wanted the car for the day, he would take his father to the market where he worked as a butcher and pick him up at the end of the day. If I wanted to drive, I had to make sure my parents didn't need the car for that day. Finally, Don bought a 1956 Chevy Bel Air. It was a decent car and got us where we wanted to go. All summer long, we rode around town with the windows down and the radio blasting. When we first heard Elvis together, Donnie would roll his eyes and say, "I know he's your favorite, but what about me?" I assured him he was number one with me. For the rest of the summer, every time Elvis's song played, he would roll his eyes, and we would laugh. We had such fun driving around in that Chevy!

Donnie sang to me in private all the time, mostly while riding in the car or alone at his house or mine. We didn't have a special song, but he would always express his feelings with a love song. That summer, Donnie got a lot of singing engagements, so he was occupied most of the time. When he wasn't busy practicing or working, we would steal some time for ourselves. I busied myself with babysitting, as that was what teenage girls did at that time.

Our town had a beautiful outdoor summer theater, which brought in top-class plays like *West Side Story* and singers such as Tom Jones and Engelbert Humperdinck. For my birthday, Don bought us tickets to see Tab Hunter, one of my favorites. Tab was a well-known actor, singer, and teen idol. Besides all that, he was blond, tanned, and good-looking. I remember debating what I would wear. I decided on a beautiful off-white spaghetti-strap dress, and I put my hair up in a French twist. After the show, Don encouraged me to have a picture taken with Tab, so I got up the courage to ask him for a photo and to tell him that we shared the same birthday. At that point, I was shaking and my knees were knocking, but I did have my picture taken with him. What a terrific evening. Spending a night out with Donnie and meeting Tab Hunter—what else could a girl want? It was the very best birthday.

As September was closing in, Don invited my parents and me to go to the Miss America pageant in Atlantic City, New Jersey, on Labor Day weekend. We drove there on a Friday after my dad finished work, checked into the motel, and dashed out for a night on the boardwalk. What an exciting, fun place. Everything was open until at least midnight. The next day, Donnie and I went on an aerial sightseeing tour of Atlantic City. The scenery was breathtaking. We could see the boardwalk, buildings, the ocean, and the beach. We went back to the motel and told my parents how great the aerial tour was. As we were describing what the pilot pointed out to us, I suddenly had a strong flash of memory of another ocean. *But what ocean?* I thought. I had never been to the ocean before this trip to Atlantic City, so I was puzzled about feeling such a strong connection. At the time, I shrugged it off and left the motel to enjoy the afternoon on the beach. But images of oceans and lakes began to haunt my dreams. During daylight hours, vivid pictures would flash through my mind of row houses made of brick with big windows and rainy, dreary weather. It was confusing, so I tried to ignore it.

That evening, we all dressed up in semiformal outfits. I wore a turquoise chiffon cocktail dress, with silver earrings and a bracelet. My mom wore a black silk cocktail dress, accessorized with a simple gold chain necklace, a bracelet, and diamond earrings. She looked so beautiful on the arm of my handsome dad in his black tuxedo. We all felt like royalty as we left the motel and headed out to dinner at Captain Starns, a famous seafood restaurant that overlooked the boardwalk and ocean. By the time we arrived at the convention center for the pageant, I was so excited I could barely speak. Our seats were right near the runway, with a perfect view of the beautiful and talented contestants. Of course, we cheered for Miss New York, but Miss Ohio won. I was thrilled to be part of this adventure, especially with Donnie by my side. I was feeling closer to him than ever by now. Our relationship was strong, and I always felt that we could be ourselves with each other.

The next day, Sunday, we went back to the boardwalk and walked around, feeling a little sad that the fabulous weekend was winding down. As Don and I passed a jewelry store, he stopped and looked carefully at the jewelry in the display window. He pulled me inside the store and went immediately to the ring section while I stopped to look at the earrings. A few minutes later, I heard him calling my name.

"Come see," he said, holding up a silver ring with a pearl. "Do you like it?"

"It's beautiful!" I felt a surge of incredible happiness when he presented the ring to me. I slipped it over my finger and promised to wear it every day.

As we strolled along the boardwalk again, we passed an

artist who was sketching portraits of people. We watched him for a long time and thought that he really captured the person's looks. Don and I decided to have him sketch our portrait. When the artist was finished, we were astonished by its beauty. We gave it to my parents, who loved it and hung it in their living room. Donnie and I took a picture of it, and I carried it in my wallet. I still have the portrait and picture today.

During the summer, I had realized that Donnie and I often had the same thoughts, often saw things the same way, and would say the same thing at the same time and finish each other's sentences. We laughed about it at first, but after awhile I wasn't laughing. I told him we seemed to be on the same wavelength all the time. He agreed. It was like two people with one brain. How could two different people from different walks of life be so similar and familiar? I didn't have an answer and was even more puzzled when we started experiencing many ESP-like moments. All I'd have to do was think about him, and the next thing I knew, the phone would ring, and he was on the other end, telling me he was thinking about me. I tried to think about this as coincidence, but the connection between us became stronger and stronger, and these moments happened all the time. Still, we didn't think much about it then and just believed this made our relationship all the more special.

New Beginnings: A Change in a Relationship

When our senior year began in September 1963, we weren't in any classes together except chorus. I was thinking about what college I might like to attend and what career to choose. My heart was set on becoming a mortician, but I had overprotective parents, and I knew the career I had hoped for was in jeopardy. They didn't want me to study in another town and talked me out of it. They suggested I choose a college near our town, but those colleges didn't offer the programs I wanted to study. My English and science teachers thought I should go into teaching these subjects, but I felt too shy about standing in front of twenty-five students and teaching them. Don had an idea, though. He said he was thinking about going to Holland to visit family, and if he decided to stay, I could stay with him there and study to become a Dutch/English interpreter. Decisions, decisions! I needed time to make my own decision about where my life was headed, and I wasn't ready to decide just yet. When he mentioned going to Holland, I again felt a funny feeling—almost an eerie, sad feeling. I also had glimpses of myself in Dutch clothing. Was I crazy? Dreaming?

Christmas came, and we were all excited about the holidays. We both planned on spending Christmas Eve and part of Christmas Day with our families. I asked him to come to my house when he could on Christmas Day so we could spend some time together. He bought me the most beautiful gift: a heart with a ruby (my birthstone) necklace. It was stunning and I treasured it. He certainly had good taste. By the way, I still have that necklace.

That winter, he received numerous offers for singing gigs, but he chose the one closest to home. He appeared there most of the winter and was making pretty good money.

In April 1964, Donnie was invited to Holland by his relatives. His uncle got him an audition for a singing part on a late-night show. He was asked to stay in Holland and was assured some jobs. He decided to return to the United States to finish school, but continued to work every show he could to save money for a return trip to Holland. We saw each other often that summer.

Before he returned to Holland in September 1964, he bought me a purple stuffed dog, which we named Van. He told me to put Van on my bed so that every night before I went to sleep, I'd think of him. I remember driving him to the airport so he could fly back to Holland. It was bittersweet. I was happy for him but sad that he was leaving. He tried to be uplifting, but I could see the sadness in his eyes. He talked about coming home for Christmas and all the things we could do when he returned. When he walked to the plane, he never looked back at me because he knew I was crying, as he was, too.

When he arrived in Holland, he called and told me about his upcoming agenda. He also suggested that I could move to Holland after I finished college. He was sure I could find a job there. Since I had just started college, I had time to think about it. As soon as he mentioned moving to Holland, I felt an uncomfortable, eerie sensation, as if I might be in some sort of danger if I went there. I did not understand this fear, but I accepted it and knew I would not be visiting Donnie, even for a short time.

I felt truly heartbroken when Donnie returned to Holland and wondered if he would end up staying or if he would ever return home. When he mentioned everything going on in his life, I knew he would probably stay in Holland. I think we both thought about marriage one day, because we would talk about it when we were dating, but as time went on, I didn't think it would work because I didn't want to live in Holland or be away from my family. And, I guess, I knew he had to concentrate on his singing career. As the months went on, he asked me several times again to visit him in Holland so I could see what it was like there. I demurred. Was I making the wrong choice?

Meanwhile, Donnie ended up receiving a lot of opportunities. A recording company signed a contract with him, he had many shows and appearances and was on his way to becoming a star. With all of that going on, I knew, down deep, he was homesick and missed me as I missed him.

I concentrated on my studies at the business school; the classes were easy, and I breezed through them. When I graduated, I would be an executive secretary. It wasn't something I really wanted to do, but I was stuck now with this career choice.

From September through December, Don and I were in constant communication by phone and mail. We still had this ESP connection going on, too. The distance between us didn't seem to matter. When December came, I started getting excited because I thought Donnie was coming home. But he had a lot of engagements already booked and didn't have the time to spend here. I was so disappointed, and so was he. We missed each other so much.

After the holidays, Don went on tour to different countries and sang with famous pop artists. He met kings, queens, princes, princesses, diplomats, and other officials. He also was cutting a new album. The life he wanted was happening. I stayed behind and wondered about what my future would bring. Little did I know then that Donnie would prove to be forever part of my life, both past and present.

Henry: True Love

M eanwhile, during the spring of 1965, I was waiting to graduate from business school and find a job as an executive secretary. Since January, I had had many job offers, but refused them because I wanted to finish school. Now it was time to decide which one I wanted to take. During the last semester, one of my friends invited me to her party. I wasn't sure about attending, but all my friends were going, so I decided to go, too. That's when I met my future husband, Henry. Henry was a handsome Italian guy, with dark, wavy hair and expressive brown eyes that made me smile whenever I looked at him. He was kind of quiet, but fun to be around. We talked for most of the evening and got to know each other; at the end of the evening, he asked me to go on a date with him. I politely refused because I still was communicating with Don.

A few weeks later, I saw Henry again at a local bar we frequented because they always had good bands and my friends and I liked to dance. He and I danced all evening and had a great time. He then asked me again for a date and I gave in—he was hard to resist! Henry was easygoing and fun to be with, and I enjoyed his company so much. He once again asked me to date him, but I wasn't sure. I did, however, tell him about Donnie. His comment about Don was "I'm here and he's there." That's what Henry was like—funny, easygoing, and confident that he would achieve his goal. That year was fun for both of us. We did everything from dancing and dining with friends, to visiting lakes in the Adirondacks and the horse races in Saratoga. I began to think less about Donnie and more about Henry. The following year, in April 1966, he asked me to marry him. *Marry? Oh my gosh!* I thought. *I'm too young to be married.* I had always wanted to be a wife and mother—some day! Was he the right man for me?

I was still communicating with Donnie, but more infrequently now. Don would always tell me to go out with my friends and have a good time, but he didn't think I would meet someone who I would consider marrying. For me, Donnie was a person I cared deeply about and felt as if I had known a long time. But Henry was right. Donnie was gone, and being with Henry made my life feel complete.

When I became engaged to Henry, Donnie and I stopped all communication. He was, however, still in touch with my parents. Even when I wasn't in contact with him, I still was experiencing ESP with him—flashes of him came to my mind, and I wondered about his singing career and what country he might be in. Within a few days, my questions were answered, because he or his parents would call my mom and tell her what was going on.

Only human, I did think about Donnie and what we once had, but he was off singing in another country, and I knew the relationship was over. I was head over heels in love with Henry and looking forward to beginning a life with him. But I also couldn't shake the feeling that Don and I were still connected somehow. *What is it with this man?* I wondered. I was experiencing even stronger episodes of déjà vu—if I walked into a local bakery or boutique, I would feel a strong sense of familiarity, as if I was used to being in that setting. I tried to dismiss these sensations so I could get on with my life. Sometimes that was quite difficult to do, as the episodes got so strong.

Donnie did return home in July 1966, three months before my marriage to Henry. He came to my house, unannounced, and stayed for about an hour. We made small talk, mostly; there was so much to say, but neither one of us said anything about our situation. Could've, should've, would've—but it didn't happen. When he left, he kissed me good-bye and told me he would write me a letter when he returned to Holland. Well, he did write a letter and told me that if things didn't work out with Henry or if I was ever unhappy, he would always be there for me. So not only did I feel connected to him, but I was also sure he felt the same way.

But my feelings for Henry were very strong. After a lot of soul searching, my instincts told me that Henry was the right man for me. He possessed all the qualities I admired: he was kind, considerate, and respectful, and a really nice person. His biggest asset was being a Good Samaritan. If anyone needed his help, he would immediately stop what he was doing to help him or her. I had no doubts about Henry. He was my destiny.

We married in October 1966. Six years later, our son, Todd, was born. He was the joy of our lives. Henry was a good father and husband, although sometimes protective. His family's needs always came first, and we had a great family life together. When discussing decisions or issues, I would always ask him what we should do or how we should handle something. Henry would always tell me to make the decision or handle the issue, because he thought that I had good instincts and would make the right choice. Sometimes I felt a bit uncomfortable about that because I felt we should make the decisions together. Henry was right, though, because my intuition was right on target for the most part, and I was able to make good decisions.

A few years later, after looking at numerous houses, we decided to build our own. Henry did most of the work himself so that the house would be customized to our liking. He chose to work a night shift so that he could work on the house during the day.

When Todd was in first grade, I returned to work in the school system and could then spend summers and vacation weeks with our son. Luckily, my parents were retired and offered to watch Todd. He would stay with them for an hour before the school bus arrived and an hour after school. He was the love of their lives, and he liked spending time with them.

During our marriage, I continued to have many déjà vu moments and flashbacks that made me wonder if I had lived a past life. One of the reasons I was able to investigate my many dreams and déjà vu moments was because my husband was so accepting of my intuitive self.

Henry supported me whenever and wherever I found answers. When we discussed my dreams and memory flashes, he would tell me that things would come together for me "at the right time." One of the right times was in the spring of 1999, when we took a trip to Charleston, South Carolina. We drove on the scenic route from Myrtle Beach to Charleston so we could see different sights. About halfway to Charleston, I noticed a plantation house that looked like the one that had appeared in my dreams since I was a child. I asked my husband to turn around so I could have a better view, and Henry was quick to oblige.

"Oh my gosh!" I said to Henry. "This is the house and yard I see in my dream!" During our marriage, whenever I told Henry about this setting from my dream, he would always say, "It must mean something." Now, here we were in front of the house I had dreamt about so often. I felt excited, as if I had just been given a wonderful gift: the dream that had haunted me for many years was a reality. What did it mean, though? It would take me many more years to find out.

When we arrived in Charleston, I continued to have flashes of memory connected to the house and could see and feel the energy of the people from the 1860s—the air felt thick and heavy to me, and I could sense shadows of people dressed in nineteenth-century styles. At one point, I actually saw my mother and father from my dream getting into a horse and buggy to go on a business trip. It was a comforting and familiar feeling, one I will never forget. After this encounter, I never had this dream again.

My memory flashes did not stop there. While we were touring parts of Charleston, we came upon some colored row houses with people riding bikes along the water, which triggered flashes of Holland. This was also a familiar feeling for me. At the time, I did not understand what significance Holland had in my past lives, but that mystery would be solved years later when I began past life regression therapy.

By the way, Henry also exhibited signs of intuition. When driving south on our trip to Charleston, we stopped in Winchester, Virginia, to eat lunch and to purchase a back signal light for the car. When we approached the city, Henry drove right to a restaurant and then to an auto parts store. I asked him if he had ever been to this city and he answered no. But he knew exactly where places were. We just looked at each other and laughed. We were both open to intuitive guidance, and it was very comforting to know Henry was also tuned in.

Henry and I liked to travel by car and explore new areas. Interestingly, all these trips were in places surrounded by water, which I have been drawn to throughout my life. We took a trip to the Florida Keys, starting at Key Largo and ending at Key West. We had to cross forty-two bridges, the longest being seven miles. Overall, we traveled 110 miles across water. Throughout this trip, I experienced many flashes of Holland—riding my bike along a canal, taking a boat trip on another ocean, and crossing bridges in a country that was familiar but that I had never visited.

One of my favorite family trips was when we took a winter vacation on the east coast of Florida. Although we had family living in various cities on the east coast and did visit them, we ultimately enjoyed being alone together. It was a time when we could revive ourselves. Todd was in high school then, and he was able to join us on his school break. We really benefitted from spending time together as a family. It was calming, not having to deal with our hectic lives at home—a nice, fun escape for all of us.

For my fiftieth birthday, Henry surprised me with a trip to Bar Harbor, Maine, and a cruise to Nova Scotia. Neither one of us had ever traveled there or been on a cruise. Bar Harbor was beautiful, and the cruise was fun—I was delighted to be able to spend so much time on the water. We met some interesting people from different states and countries who shared many fascinating travel stories with us.

As the years rolled on, I was busy working, being a wife and mother, cooking, cleaning, and taking care of the house, so I didn't have much free time for myself. Every once in a while, especially when I was driving alone or riding by Donnie's house, our high school, or our summer theater, I would think and wonder about Don. Now and then my mom talked about him and said she wondered what happened to him. Yes, we both wondered what he was doing, how he was, and where he was. Neither one of us ever saw his relatives, so we were really out of touch.

Mom and I were surprised that he never tried to contact us. He must have come home to visit his family here at some point, right? Wherever he was in the world, we both always wished him the very best in life.

Transition: Learning to Live Alone

enry and I finally retired, Henry four years before me. Our dream was to live in Florida for six months during the winter. We both were so tired of the winters in New York. That plan seemed perfect for us, as we traveled to Florida many times and enjoyed living in a condo in Sarasota. But during the summer of 2000, our dreams were shattered. Henry suffered a massive heart attack and died. I was beside myself and felt like I was in the twilight zone. It was a nightmare for both Todd and me, with Todd losing his dad and me losing my husband of thirty-four years. Henry was the one person we could always rely on. He was our rock! Deep depression followed.

The past five years have been difficult for me as well. I lost my mom and dad and two close aunts. I had emergency bowel reconstruction surgery and was in the hospital for a month. My recovery was difficult after all that. I was really surprised I didn't have a nervous breakdown. I wasn't totally alone though. I had my son, Todd; a close cousin, Joe, and his wife, Joan; my friends Mary Anne and

Marjorie; and others who were supportive. They all helped me to get through that painful time in my life.

One day in May 2001, after spending my first winter alone, a friend and I decided to attend a message circle. I had been feeling terribly sad and missing Henry so much. I thought perhaps I could receive a message from him. For years, I had felt an intuitive tug each time I passed by the Psychic Development Center in my neighborhood. *I should try that out,* I'd think, feeling curious about what the center offered. My friend and I both felt open to the possibilities. She wanted to hear from her grandmother but was also realistic and didn't want to get her hopes up. She warned, "Let's not be discouraged if we don't hear a message this time." We felt scared, but together we took that first step. I am so glad I did because it has opened up my life in ways I never could have imagined!

When the circle began, the psychic medium who was organizing it told us that some of us might receive a message and some might not. As we began, the psychic was quiet for a few minutes and then gave the message "Your husband can hear you." My friend and I were astounded; we both knew the psychic was receiving a message from Henry. I had asked Henry an important question the winter after he died but had received no answer—until this moment.

In message circles, the psychic is drawn to one person in the circle, and this psychic was drawn to me. He asked if my husband had passed recently and whether he had passed from a heart attack. Some people might be skeptical about the authenticity of these questions, but I was not, especially after the psychic asked if we had wintered in a first-floor condo in Florida and then went on to describe our condo in detail. "Did you ever ask your husband a question in that condo and he never answered you?" the psychic said.

The winter after Henry passed, I was at the condo,

feeling lonely and missing my Henry. I was sitting in the living room, looking through the lanai into the backyard and thinking about how much Henry had loved this place. It was then that I asked aloud, "Hon, can you hear me, and can you give me a message?" I just wanted to know that he was with me.

Before that evening, I often received signals that I thought were from Henry. The phone would ring and no one was there; lights would go on and off. While I felt depressed at that time, I was not taking medication; I had a great support system that I could rely on to get me through this difficult time. In fact, Joe and Joan were staying with me in Florida for six weeks during that time and had witnessed some of these events. It was not a matter of wishful thinking; Henry was keeping in touch with me, and when I heard that message from the psychic, it confirmed for me what I was already experiencing.

Two months later, I went back to another message circle and received another message from Henry, who said, "Yes, I can hear you, and I love you. Don't worry—when you go back to Florida you will have a good support system of people who will become good friends." Henry was right, for I kept the condo for another four years and enjoyed many wonderful winters with some very dear friends. Henry's message to me became a source of comfort and healing and gave me the strength to go on and make a life on my own.

In March 2004, my granddaughter, Cassie, was born. Oh, I was so ecstatic when she arrived. I now had a purpose in life and that was to take care of her during the day when my son and daughter-in-law worked. Cassie was a joy to watch, and I enjoyed every phase of her new life. If only Henry could have been here to see her. But then I realized he did. When Cassie was a toddler, she would point to his picture and say, "Papa." No one ever mentioned him to her, but yet she seemed to know him. I think she could "see" him, as Cassie is very intuitive.

Todd and his wife, Jen, decided Cassie needed to be with other children and enrolled her in a nursery school. She loved playing and learning with other children, but I missed her—missed her a lot.

That's when I decided to turn my life around. I was existing, not living, after Henry died. I had grieved for some time, but now I decided I wanted to do something meaningful to help other people in various ways. I thought about volunteer work. Different organizations always need volunteers in some way or another. There were hospitals, missions, children's homes, animal shelters, food banks, etc. All were important; I just couldn't make a choice. I felt frozen, without purpose, but still not able to choose the direction my life would go in.

In May 2004, all that changed. When my friend and I went back to the center, we met therapist healers who were practicing Reiki and Therapeutic Touch (TT) on the circle attendees. Although I did not know it then, I soon discovered how energy practices work. The Reiki practitioners treat the whole person by balancing the chakras and channeling the universal energy where it is needed by laying their hands on a person to change the energy flow and allow for self-healing. In Therapeutic Touch, the practitioners use their hands to move energy, and it is scientifically proven to heal the person in many ways. I watched for a while until I was comfortable enough to try it. A woman in her early forties did a Reiki healing on me. After everyone had her turn, I went back to her for a Therapeutic Touch healing. Both made me feel really good—relaxed and much less stressed, with a clear mind. Before this, I had only had acupuncture done the previous winter. That was a relaxing experience, too, and offered me an unexpected bonus: during the session I experienced visions and images of what I now realize were past lives, such as seeing myself in Egypt or ice-skating on a canal in Holland. After experiencing acupuncture, I was open to exploring other alternative therapies. I was curious about how they would help me understand what these images were all about.

The next time I went to a circle, I met Shelly, a Reiki and TT practitioner who did a healing on me. I again felt wonderfully relaxed. When I learned that she did healings on people in their homes, I immediately asked her to come to my house. A few days later, Shelly gave me a great Reiki healing at my home, and she was excellent at it. As soon as she began the healing session, I felt energy flowing through my body. It's funny, but I was dog sitting for my son at the time, and when Shelly began the Reiki, the dog came over and sat at my feet and stayed there throughout the whole session. When the session was over, he moved back over to the other side of the room. It was clear to me that the dog wanted some of that great stream of energy I was feeling.

After the session, Shelly and I talked about classes on alternative therapies, and she promised to drop off information on classes to me. Just as she was leaving, she seemed to hesitate.

"I have something to tell you," she said. "I saw a man around you when I was doing the healing. Hovering over you. Really nice man. Who was that?"

Shelly was describing my husband. I felt a great sense of comfort knowing he was close by.

Within a few days, I had all the information I needed on teachers and where classes were being taught. Because I had to put myself out there, I decided a smaller class would be better for me. Taking that first step was unsettling, to say the least. I felt very shy, but was intrigued and open to the healing. I was ready to make a big change in my life. I wanted to do something worthwhile to help other people, and that desire gave me the confidence to try something new. For the first time in a long time, I was excited about the possibilities I could create in my life.

In September 2005, I enrolled in my first Usui Reiki I class with Elaine, a teacher at a local high school. Don't forget, it had been years since I enrolled in a class, and I was feeling somewhat nervous. But Elaine was a dynamic, caring teacher, and her positive energy and welcoming nature made my usual shyness disappear entirely! She held small classes in her comfortable home, where we could relax and easily discuss a variety of topics. Elaine had a wide range of personal experiences—everything from insomnia, emotional traumas, and aches and pains in the body to healing the eyesight of a young boy, which she discussed openly with us. Knowing the fundamentals of Reiki was good, but hearing about life experiences was great. When she administered our first attunement, I felt my crown, heart, and palm chakras open up. Chakras are spinning wheels of energy, and colors are associated with each one. Since I felt my crown, heart, and palm chakras, I was seeing colors of white and green. I felt some pressure and tingling and a sense of peace, energy, and alertness. I felt like a flower taking in water.

After that first attunement, I began experiencing more visions and past life memories, as well as moments of psychic awareness. I had a vision and past life memory of Don and me playing kickball in a place I had never seen before. In class, Elaine asked me if I had any color awareness, and I told her I kept seeing the color purple around her. She then told me she was sending me this color.

In Elaine's class, we would often practice on each other to learn the healing method, and I always felt secure with her and knew that I was never in any danger. In fact, once during a practice Reiki session, another student forgot to ground me; when I got up off the table, I felt dizzy. Elaine immediately balanced my energy and grounded me.

Reiki I was my first step toward becoming a healer. I really fell in love with Reiki and was eager to take more classes and learn as much as I could about this healing process. After I finished the first class with Elaine, I enrolled in her Reiki II and Reiki III classes as well.

One year later, in September 2006, I expanded my knowledge of healing therapies when Shelly encouraged me to enroll in a Therapeutic Touch class with Sue, a teacher she highly recommended. Sue first got involved in TT after watching a video of Dolores Krieger, RN, PhD, doing a Therapeutic Touch treatment on a little boy in the early 1990s. To Sue, it just "felt so logical." When she saw some of the research related to this area, she realized that this was a treatment that combined the best of both worlds— allopathic medicine and complementary therapies. Since about 2000, Sue has spent time studying and teaching with Dee Krieger and many other great Therapeutic Touch teachers and practitioners. Sue encouraged her students to concentrate and practice TT in order to become excellent healers. One of the most amazing experiences I had in Sue's class was when we were taking turns treating each other. I was observing the healing technique of another student, and I happened to see the healed person's aura (energy field). From that moment on, I have been able to see auras. Sue's class taught me above and beyond the requirements and set me on my path as a healer.

I went on to earn my Master Reiki certificate in 2010. When I was ready to enroll in the Usui Reiki Master class and Karuna Reiki, Elaine had moved to a different state, but I knew another teacher, Al, from the Reiki therapy work that we did together as volunteers in hospitals and nursing homes. Al was a terrific teacher, too. I have taken many classes and workshops with Al over the years and have learned a lot from him. He helped me learn how to receive messages and interpret them, fine-tune my healing practices, and use Reiki to its fullest potential. One of the things I liked best about Al as a teacher was that he taught us to be sensitive to the needs and feelings of others. His Karuna Reiki class taught me a more intense form of healing, and I believe it strengthened my healing abilities tremendously.

Al first learned about Reiki when his wife began practicing it, but he always felt physically uncomfortable if he was in the same room when she was practicing. He went to conventions and expositions on his interest in dowsing, and whenever Reiki was being practiced, he had to leave because he couldn't stand the energy. Finally, he decided that he needed to deal with his discomfort with Reiki energy. He talked with a Reiki Master, who told him that if he became attuned, he would not feel this bad energy. Al went to a Reiki session, where he received his first attunement. During the session, he felt a strong sensation of cleansing and change in his being. He went on to achieve master levels in both Reiki and Therapeutic Touch and taught them to others, including me.

Over five years, I took numerous Reiki and Therapeutic Touch classes and found great joy in helping people heal. If you are thinking about learning these therapies, just know that you don't need to be "special" to be a healer. Healers are conduits for the universal energy to flow through. Healing has been known to clear blockages, treat illnesses, and ease emotional stress. A person needs to be whole in body, mind, and spirit.

In 2006, I began doing Therapeutic Touch at a local nursing home and Reiki at a local hospital on a volunteer basis. I also volunteered healings at fitness centers, wellness and healing centers, and in homes. People responded well to these alternative therapies. Doing TT as a volunteer at different places gave me the practice I needed to work with different energies from different people. For instance, I learned how to be open to messages while healing so that I could more effectively create positive energy for the person. Sometimes I could feel a spirit around the person urging me to tell them to do something relevant to a decision in their life, job, or relationship, or even about their car or something they needed to fix in their life.

After a few months of volunteering, Sue asked me if I was interested in volunteering on the hospice floor of a local hospital. My immediate reaction was "I can't do this! It'd be too hard to give healings on such vulnerable patients." But Sue encouraged me. I mustered up my courage and decided to give it a try. My first day, I went in to see a patient whom the nursing staff had warned me was "difficult to deal with."

"Hi, Fred," I said as I entered his room. "How are you doing? Would you like a treatment?"

"I don't think so," he replied, looking slightly bothered by my intrusion.

I kept talking to him, even though he didn't answer. Sometimes patients don't want therapy—they just want to talk. So I tried talking to him about NASCAR, one of my favorite sports. He sparked up! After discussing NASCAR with him for a few minutes, Fred said, "You know something? I think I'll take that therapy now."

Another time I did a healing on a woman who was having trouble with her leg and foot from complications from diabetes. I went to her home every week for a while, doing a total-body healing. As I was moving around her, with my hands near her body, I felt something in her chest area and other leg. She said that leg hurt her. To me, it felt like congestive heart failure, but not being a doctor, I would not tell her this. I instead told her that she was putting pressure on the other leg and that she should tell her doctor about the leg that hurt. When she did and he ran tests, he found congestive heart failure. I was happy that she then had a correct diagnosis.

When I offered these therapies at fitness centers, people who just wanted to try it often came for healings. I found lots of different areas in people that were not right. For example, if someone was under a lot of emotional stress, I would receive a message about the circumstances behind it and then could focus my healing therapy on relaxing his or her mind and spirit. When I could feel that a person had a headache, a message would come through about why they had a headache, and I would then focus my attention in that area. Or, if they were experiencing sore or pulled muscles, Reiki or TT would make them feel better after about fifteen minutes.

In nursing and assisted living homes, the elderly people we treated came every week. They would always tell us that the areas that hurt felt much better after our therapies. We could usually detect areas on them that needed attention. I like to body scan a person first because I can feel what areas of his or her body need help. For example, I might sense they had sore muscles or back and knee problems and work specifically on those areas. There was one patient I just loved. He always asked for me and would tell me, "After you did that healing, I slept really well all week."

Our volunteer group always felt good about helping the patients feel better and improving their quality of life. I liked knowing that I could make a difference, even in a small way.

Every year in October, my healing group is invited to participate in the nurses' recognition day. The day starts with a luncheon, followed by a few speeches and then relaxing therapies such as Reiki, TT, and massages treatments. I thoroughly enjoy doing healings on these special nurses who give of themselves every day by helping their patients. Some of these nurses perform Reiki and TT on patients and find that it helps them as they undergo operations and begin healing.

I have discovered my purpose in life, a purpose that is fulfilling in so many ways. Learning how to give energy healings has been the first step toward a greater awareness of my own intuition and my soul's progression.

Past Lives: Tapping into My Psychic Abilities

A s I continued to provide TT and Reiki therapies, I began getting messages, thoughts, and feelings about people I was treating. I was used to Henry giving me messages, like blinking lights off and on in the house, coughing, sitting on the bed, and especially finding me a parking spot. When I was alone at night and in bed but not sleeping, I would feel the bed move, like someone was sitting down on Henry's side of the bed. I would lie still, to see if it might happen again. Most of the time, it did. I knew, just knew, that it was Henry checking on me.

Henry helped me in other ways, too. When Joan and Joe were visiting me in Sarasota, Florida, during the winter months, finding a parking spot was always difficult. One day, when we went shopping at St. Armand's Circle, we rode around for a while, searching for a spot. Then Joan said, "Hey, Hank, we need a parking spot." Immediately after she said this, one appeared. We laughed and said, "Thanks, Hank." She continued to ask for Henry's help, and we had a parking spot every time. When in need, I know I can count on Hank for a parking spot, because whenever I ask, one always appears.

While I was doing laundry one day at home in New York, I heard coughing in the basement near my husband's workbench. It sounded like Henry, but I thought it was Todd, because he often uses that workbench to fix equipment. When I called, "Todd, is that you?" there was no answer. I have heard this coughing a few times, and now I just say, "Hi, hon."

Although I was used to getting messages from him, receiving messages about other people was quite a different story. I could feel the positive or negative energy around them and sometimes see a person standing by them. But knowing things about them was freaky! It took a little while to get used to, but soon enough I grew comfortable with these energies and messages and would focus the healing energy on promoting people's self-healing.

Looking back, I realize now that because of the Reiki and TT work I was doing, I had completely opened myself up to receiving spirit messages and psychic energy. I also did a lot of meditating during this time, which was actually pretty easy for me. I looked forward to meditation time, because it increased my awareness and sensitivity to psychic moments, especially because I began receiving images and thoughts about Don and me in another setting. I had vivid images of working at a bakery, riding my bike near water, and going to the beach, doing most of this as a teenager with Don—but these were in places I had never been before, certainly not with Don in this present life. I was growing more and more certain that this setting was another lifetime, and I wanted to know more about it.

My psychic abilities became more developed as I continued to learn from other energy practitioners. This group included some interesting and knowledgeable people, many of whom were intuitives, psychic mediums, astrologers, and authors. They all have been great mentors for me. My friend Pat is a gifted psychic medium and can do past life regressions and readings. She has been extremely important in my life, because during my readings and PLR, she has guided me in the right direction. She has always been correct with everything she has said to me. Pat has been the one to help me unravel happenings in this life and in my past lives. Interestingly, Pat and all the other psychics I consulted with gave me the same information about being connected to a light-haired man who was in the entertainment business and from whom I was separated by a great distance.

Most of these people did message circles and always invited me to attend. My friend Shelly would have circles at her house, only inviting six to eight people she knew. Shelly conducted the circle, and I received some great messages from Henry. "I'm still wearing shorts" was one that made me laugh. He wore shorts all the time, even in the winter. He also sent me the message "Our granddaughter will be gifted in many ways." Cassie was born within the year.

During circles, I was at first too shy to give anyone a message, but Shelly encouraged me to speak up. She would always say, "Don't sit on anything, and trust what you're getting." Even though some of the messages sounded weird to me, the people receiving them understood them fully. When people confirmed the messages, I felt more confident.

Encouraged by my other friends in the group, I attended more circles and received more messages. The more circles I attended, the more messages I received, and they were always very clear. During the meditation at these circles, I began getting more blips about Don and me, especially of sitting at an ocean beach, riding my bike near water, and walking on flat land near water.

When I confided in Shelly about the messages I was

receiving regarding Don and the blips I was getting about our past lives together, she suggested I try a past life regression session without hypnosis. I followed her advice.

I recalled my first two past lives through dreams and consultations with a reputable psychic medium whom I first met in her New Age shop in Sarasota, Florida. When I walked into the shop, I was taken back. It was a beautiful place, and I loved everything in it. Lourdes, the owner, introduced herself and told me a little about her store.

Lourdes had many unique items, and the first ones I noticed were the beautiful Herkimer diamonds. While talking with Lourdes about these stones, I asked her how she had acquired them. She told me that she and her husband take a trip to Herkimer, New York, every year to purchase them. I laughed and told her I lived about an hour away from Herkimer and that I had been to the Herkimer Diamond Mine several times. It is a fascinating place, and visitors are able to mine these crystals themselves or buy them at the store. The Herkimer diamond, actually a double-pointed quartz crystal, is thought by many to have holistic qualities and metaphysical properties such as harmony and awareness, which can alleviate tension, enhance clairvoyance, and store information. The crystal can be clear, cloudy, and smoky or have impurities. Because of all the good properties and beauty of this stone, it is my favorite. I have had a few pieces of jewelry made from them. My favorite is a necklace that seems to carry good energy. I wear it frequently, especially when I am healing someone.

I enjoyed looking at Native American items at Lourdes's shop, especially the crystals, gemstones, oils, and jewelry. She also carried other interesting objects, such as dream catchers, decorative pipes, wall hangings, smudge bowls and sticks, feathers, and fans. Lourdes also had a variety of books, including volumes about the healing of the earth, astronomy, astrology, spiritualism, science, tarot-card reading, and self-help psychic-medium development, which she directed me to specifically. She thought I just needed to fine-tune my psychic-medium abilities. Those books did offer guidance and information that was useful, especially *Power of the Soul* by John Holland. This book enabled me to tap into my soul.

Lourdes told me she was a psychic medium and that she did readings at her shop. She also mentioned having a psychic fair that coming weekend and invited me to attend. Well, I did attend, and I met many intriguing people, including an astrologer, a massage therapist, an energy healer, a tarot card reader, and psychics. At Lourdes's psychic fair, she also did aura readings and chakra and energy healings.

I passed on a reading at the fair, but told Lourdes that I would love a reading from her at her shop. I was very comfortable with Lourdes; I felt like we had known each other for a long time. When I returned to her shop a few days later, I was excited about what I might learn. As she was doing my reading, she asked if I was tied to Egyptian things. I told her yes, that I had often dreamed of an Egyptian life and was now getting stronger flashes about this life and would like to piece it together. She said to return in a few days and she would do a past life regression reading. We then uncovered one of my past lives, which brought me back to ancient Egypt. I envisioned this life with mind pictures and images, like a slide show.

I saw myself during Cleopatra's rule, when women were ahead of their time. They had the same rights as men and could rule a country. They also could own their own businesses, be in entertainment, and be wives and mothers, which always came first. My husband and I had an arranged marriage, which luckily turned out to be a good one. I also knew that if the marriage hadn't worked out, I could seek a divorce and remarry. He was a good man, though, and we produced a beautiful daughter. We both were interested in astronomy, and my husband taught me many things about it. I saw myself owning a perfume business, with about twenty people working for me. Eventually, after years of learning, my daughter ran this business, and I retired.

In this present life, I am fascinated with Egyptian history and artifacts and the intelligence and knowledge of the Egyptian civilization. While wintering in Florida about three years ago, Marjorie and I went to an Egyptian exhibit in Sarasota. I had a strong sense that I seen these items before and had actually used them. I walked around this exhibit four times and was struck by feelings of familiarity. The next day I returned by myself and just slowly looked and stopped at everything displayed.

I am also very interested in astronomy and have visited the planetarium in Bradenton, Florida, several times. Oftentimes they have amateur astronomers outside in the parking lot with their telescopes, explaining the stars and planets. I am drawn in this life to the same interests as in my previous Egyptian life.

The following year, Lourdes and I worked together again to uncover my first past life. Since I had been dreaming about this life for a long time, the regression process was quite easy. We pieced together events within this past life that now made more sense to me, as you will soon see.

My session with Lourdes was really interesting. I was brought back to the time when Abraham Lincoln was president, March 4, 1861, to April 15, 1865. For me, it was like watching a video of my life. I saw the white house with green shutters that I saw with Henry during our trip to Charleston. It seemed like a big plantation house with a long driveway and beautifully landscaped yard. Outside, in front of the house on the lawn, my two sisters and I were playing "Ring around the Rosie." We were about five, six, and seven years old. The two girls seemed so familiar. I then saw our parents. Our mother was blonde and beautiful, and our father had dark hair and was very handsome. He was a businessman and often liked our mother to accompany him on business trips. We were sad because they were leaving on a trip, and we were saying our good-byes. I also saw our mammy. Oh, how we loved her. She was like our second mother and treated us so well. I remember her feeding us great meals and making sure we dressed up when our parents were due home. How could I know this life—my parents, sisters, mammy, and house—as a child? I would dream this over and over.

Because of this dream, and with the help of regression therapy, I realized that my sisters then are my two best friends, Mary Anne and Marjorie, in this life now. The two of them are sisters, and we have been friends since we were babies. Also, I lived in a green and white house in this present life. I realize now that this is probably why I have been drawn to the South and loved reading about and drawing Abraham Lincoln.

After learning about these first two past lives with the help of Lourdes, I knew I had two more past lives because of the blips and images I was receiving through meditation and déjà vu moments. I did a past life regression session with Al, and it clarified a lot for me. Interestingly, these lives did involve Don. Learning about them helped me understand all those déjà vu moments I had experienced as a teenager that I had tried to ignore, such as the many times I had flashes of water or riding my bike along a canal. In my third life regression session with Al, which was more like a blip on a movie screen, Donnie and I lived in North Holland, he as a girl, and me as a boy. We were neighbors, and we often played together. We lived near lots of water, including the North Sea, lakes, rivers, and canals.

We rode our bikes all around and past many dikes and windmills. I also remember that Dutch people liked their privacy and didn't always invite you into their homes. One more thing—neither of us liked Dutch food. We thought it was too bland.

In this present life, I was a bit of a tomboy when I was younger. I rode my bike all the time and could keep up with any of the boys in the neighborhood or even beat them at a game. My mom always said I should have been born a boy.

When I think of Holland, I see tulips, wooden shoes, windmills, dikes, Rembrandt, and Van Gogh, but what I really see in my subconscious is something quite different: I am in concentration camps with crowds of people, being taken away at gunpoint by the Nazis, who are separating me from my family. I dream the same dreams repeatedly, and they are as vivid as real life. Once I had done a fourth past life regression session with Al, I understood better where these memories were originating from. In this past life, Donnie and I were twins, him a boy and me a girl. We lived in Germany through WWI, from 1914 to 1919. During this war between the Allies (including Great Britain, France, Russia, the United States, Italy, and Japan) and the Central Powers (the German Empire, the Austro-Hungarian Empire, and the Ottoman Empire), our father joined the army, and we were afraid we wouldn't see him again and cried bitterly when he left. Due to the lack of men, women (ages seventeen to sixty) had to work in factories for as long as sixteen hours a day to produce weapons and ammunition. Our mother worked in a factory, and we were left with relatives. When we turned seventeen, we had to work in a factory, too.

My fifth past life was pieced together by a past life regression session and a past life reading with my friend Pat. And yes, Don was a major part of this life. We were teenagers living in a small, peaceful village in North Holland. Our parents owned shops next to each other and every day, after school, he and I would ride our bikes to the shops to help out. My parents owned a bakery and his parents, a clothing store. We all were good friends, and eventually Don and I started dating. On the weekends, both of our families often went to visit relatives in Flanders, Belgium. It was fun going there, and they always made us a meal. My mother brought baked goods from our bakery. The meal usually consisted of seafood, especially mussels, or steak, French fries, and a salad, and a delicious chocolate dessert.

But when WWII started and the Nazis took control of Holland, everything changed. Don and I knew our parents were in the Dutch resistance, and if the Germans caught them, we could all be shot or sent to concentration camps.

Before the war started, we were under the impression that Holland would remain a neutral country, but of course, the Nazis couldn't let that happen. They ended up stealing our food supply and rationing it back to us. Dutch people realized they were in trouble. The Nazis also tried to recruit Dutch men into their army. One day the Germans came to our town and went inside every house looking for men. When our fathers were located, the Nazis put them on a truck and sent them to Germany, probably to work in their war factories. Our shops were closed, and our mothers, Don, and I were taken to a concentration camp, never to be seen or heard from again. I recently had a dream that I was shot in the stomach and left to die. Don was made to watch. In this present life, I had bowel issues, and my bowel burst; I'm sure this was related to my previous life in which I died from the bullet wound, which caused infection.

So, in these past lives with Don, we never made it

through our teens, were reincarnated quickly, and were reborn. In this present life, almost dying at rebirth, Donnie was reincarnated in 1945 in Holland to Dutch parents. Almost dying at rebirth myself, I chose to be reincarnated in 1946 in the United States to non-Dutch parents.

Doesn't it seem odd that Don and I ended up living in the same area surrounded by Dutch-named cities, attended the same high school, became friends, and dated in this present life? And once again, our lives together were cut short from one another, only not by death.

Donnie: Reconnecting with My Soul Mate

T he mystery of Donnie's current whereabouts started to unravel while I was in Florida during the winter of 2012, staying with my best friends, Mary Anne and Marjorie. A friend of Marjorie's introduced us to her sister, Lois, who lives in Holland. As we were talking, I asked her if she knew Don. She said she did and asked how I knew him. She then went onto a Dutch website and translated information about him and his career for me. She commented that he sounded like a nice person and that he did a lot of charity work. Lois encouraged me to contact him.

Contact him? How would I do that? I wondered. The idea intrigued me, especially because talking with Don again is on my bucket list. But more than that, he is my soul connection, and I believe we have some spiritual healing to do. When I returned home to New York in May, I was curious about Donnie and went on his English websites. Those websites kept bringing me into other sites, but I saw nothing personal—no address, phone number, or other contact information. I gave up a little at that point. I also didn't know if Joy and Chuck were still in this area. I knew I could try to contact them to find out about Don, but something was holding me back.

In the meantime, one of my friends suggested I join Facebook. I did, but didn't use it that often. One day, when I went in on one of Don's websites, I saw he was online. *Great,* I thought. *I might be able to contact him this way.* I sent him a vague message, but I knew he would know it was me. Anyway, two weeks went by and no reply. Did he not receive it? Did he not want to contact me? Did he not remember me? *Oh no,* I thought. Maybe he was on vacation or too busy. All of these thoughts raced through my mind. I tried everything I could think of, because I did not want to go through *could've, would've, should've.*

On July 1, 2012, I was on my last mission to contact Don. I had gathered up my courage and was determined not to fail this time. I went into one his websites, which brought me to another, and another, but found no personal information. Just as I was ready to give up, his mailing address, e-mail address, and phone number appeared. At the time, I found myself wondering if he would display all this information on a website. But then I thought about e-mailing him. *No,* I told myself, *I went through this already with Facebook.* After thinking it over, I decided to call him. I kept telling myself it probably wasn't the right number anyway. I contacted an international operator, who told me how to dial this number. When I placed the call, a man answered.

"Hello, is this Don?" I said.

"Yes, who is this?" he replied. I told him, and he said, "Oh my gosh, is it really you, Jan, and how are you?"

The excitement of reaching each other after forty-some years was overwhelming for both of us. I could hear it in his voice, and he certainly could hear it in mine. We talked for an hour or so about our families, school, and our trips to New York City and Atlantic City. Talking with him seemed familiar; we picked up so easily that I felt like we had never been separated. Our conversation was over too quickly, however, as Donnie told me he had to leave for a gig.

I did have a chance to ask him about the Facebook message. He said he never received it. He then gave me his personal e-mail address and asked me to e-mail him so that he would have mine. He asked me where I lived and was surprised to hear that I was in the same area. He mentioned stopping by my parents' house a few times when he came back for a visit, but no one ever came to the door. He didn't realize that my parents had passed on. He also mentioned that his sister and brother-in-law still lived in this area, too. Interestingly, Donnie lives in Wageningen, one of the cities where German forces surrendered in 1945 in our past life.

We e-mail frequently to keep in touch, and he often sends me videos of Holland, especially music videos of him singing. Donnie's voice is as rich and beautiful as I remember, and he still seems to enjoy singing and performing. When I watch the videos, I feel like I am back in a nightclub watching him perform. The picturesque backgrounds of these videos show Holland at its best. Interestingly, when I see row houses made of brick or cement with large windows and doors, a memory of me living there surfaces. And when I see buildings with beautiful architecture that look like castles, I feel like I've seen them before. My memory is really jogged by a drawbridge or a cement bridge over a canal or river. I can place myself there, looking at the canal houses, bicycling, or walking over the bridge and ice-skating on the canal. Everything feels and looks familiar to me. These scenarios have appeared many times in my dreams, flashes, and past life regression sessions.

Although Don invited me to visit him in Holland, I am

not quite ready to go back to the place where I experienced such terrible events. But even if I don't travel there, I am convinced that I have had past lives in this country with Don. Donnie and I chose to come back together for three past lives, plus this present one. The trauma of cutting off all ties with each other for so many years has not been good for us. Only Don and I can fix this. We need to stay in touch, stay connected. It's time for healing. We are planning a reunion when he comes to the United States for a visit. I know that it will happen all in good time: Jan and Donnie, together again—two hearts, one soul!

Intuition: Everyone Has It

Hindus, Buddhists, ancients Greeks, and other ancient civilizations believed in the rebirth of souls. But Christianity has rejected reincarnation and past lives since 553 AD. The Roman Empire ordered bishops to vote on the belief of reincarnation. But one of the emperors and his wife wanted reincarnation taken out of the Bible. The Roman bishops were so afraid to vote against the emperor, fearing death, that instead of keeping reincarnation in the Bible, they voted against it. Consequently, all Bibles were burned and rewritten.

I was raised Roman Catholic and was expected to follow the teachings of the church without question. We believed in an afterlife—that when you die, your soul will go to heaven or hell for eternity. Catholicism rejects reincarnation and the possibility of past lives. Catholicism also focuses on Judgment Day as a way to control people, encourage them to do good deeds, and live a good life. But scriptures are often vague and open to interpretation, and therefore conflict arises over which interpretation is correct. These conflicts create chasms in our lives, and some religions seem to be failing people today, especially young people.

I believe God is really an energy force in the universe. In fact, although we think our physical bodies are solid masses, they are actually made up of neutrons, protons, electrons, and energy. And our souls are energy, too. If more people understood universal energy and the ways we are each connected to one another through our soul energy, they would be more attuned to their intuition.

We humans are more intuitive than we realize. Everyone has the gift of intuition, that inner knowing, though some more than others. Luckily, I have had this gift since a child. The sense of a gut feeling has guided me to many good decisions in my life. The next time your inner voice talks to you, listen. It's a start.

Everyone is born with six senses, five that we are aware of—seeing, hearing, smelling, tasting, and feeling—and one we're not so aware of: connecting to the spirit world. Each of our senses works with the energy of the universe. When I started going to message circles and receiving messages from spirits, usually by thoughts and images, I knew they could communicate with me and I with them. Having been raised Roman Catholic, I was programmed with fear and denial in this area. At a young age, the church told us this sixth sense went against God and was the work of the devil, so I tried to ignore this sense. For many children, if they mentioned anything about this to their family, they would be told they were imagining things or feeling overtired. Thankfully, my parents never said this to me.

Actually, I knew my mom was psychic. Her ability to predict what would happen seemed a natural part of my family life. When I asked her how she could predict events, she would shrug her shoulders and say that she "just knew." I saw her intuition in action one summer day when she was making grape jelly. She was worried, because the last time she had made it, a friend of hers had died. "I don't have a good feeling about this," she told me. Later that day, a close relative died. Moments such as this taught me to pay attention to my intuition.

My mother was also the first person who introduced the idea of karma to me. Her favorite expression was "What goes around comes around." How right she was! I have taken her life lessons to heart.

It took awhile, but I eventually reprogrammed myself to let go of my religion's denial of the sixth sense. Over time, I let my good intuition take over; once I got through this, everything was easier for me. I could see, hear, and smell spirits (sometimes orbs), and even could be touched by them. I got shoved one time by a spirit, but in a friendly way, like the spirit was trying to say, "Hey, don't you know I'm behind you?" I guess I was tuned into them, so to speak.

During meditation, I finally connected with my spirit guide, who I came to understand was once human and had experienced a life similar to mine. I asked him if he could help me with emotional healing because I was having a difficult time with healing from the loss and separation in my life. Slowly, I started feeling better and stronger. Also, I suddenly became aware of messages that nudged me in a good direction by providing me with inspirational guidance that helped me heal. For example, I have loved music all my life, and I wanted to share my interest with my granddaughter. When I babysat her when she was young, we liked to listen to music from *The Lion King*, with "The Circle of Life" being one of our favorites. The words reminded me that we were all part of the circle of birth, growth, death, and rebirth, and I began to think about being more resilient, even while dealing with all of my sorrows. Another favorite song was "To Where You Are" by Josh Groban. It reminded me of Henry, and I cried every time I heard it; the words and music helped me believe that Henry was close and that he was watching over me. During this time, I also began watching television shows such as *Ghost Whisperer* and *Medium,* both of which got me interested in developing my psychic abilities. As I became aware of this guidance, I realized I could ask my spirit guide to help me in any way, and he would lead me to answers. I knew I needed to understand this "spirit stuff" for a reason. My knowledge has led me to past life regression sessions, and I have uncovered some of my past physical and psychological problems.

The connection between the memory flashes of my early years and the psychic exploration later on is tied into my fear of separation and dealing with death and being left alone. Exploring those memories through PLR has uncovered my fears from previous lives. I have painful memories of the wars, of separations from my family, and of death. These two fears, separation and death, need to be addressed, and I am learning to deal with these issues in this lifetime. I have learned to treasure, love, and stay close to family. I am also dealing better with being alone and feel that I'm slowly progressing. If I had followed my desire to become a mortician after high school, I might have had an easier time dealing with death; perhaps that is why I was drawn to this profession. Henry was definitely a part of that learning process: in addition to being supportive of my intuition, his death has also taught me much about myself and has helped me deal with my fears of being alone. I am curious about what role Henry played in one of my previous lives, and I look forward to uncovering it as I continue to explore these questions.

Don and I had violent deaths and were reborn quickly, and I believe that is true of anyone who experiences a sudden, traumatic end. Also, people can be female in one life and male in another—a different race, a different religion, a different everything. And on a personal level, you usually hang around with the same people from one lifetime to another. It's like "Oh, I know this soul."

Past lives are spiritual journeys toward merging with the universal consciousness. We return again and again and live lives connected to ones previously lived. Usually, friends and family members are different people in a past life. An event in your past life could be preventing something in your life today. Some people suffer from phobias, fatigue, thoughts of suicide, and nightmares due to a past life experience. These need to be addressed in this life.

As far as soul mates are concerned, I absolutely believe in them, especially with reincarnation. My soul mate and I have lived three past lives together but as different people. Having a soul mate is a spiritual relationship. It doesn't have to be a romantic love, but love, comfort, compatibility, and a psychic connection are involved. Twin souls or twin flames are on the same frequency and make you feel like one soul. This relationship can last for many lifetimes, spiritually. There are several reasons a soul mate could choose to connect with you, such as a particular lesson that needs to be learned, love, debt, soul growth, or the aid of another soul. It is possible for two souls to come together again and again due to a promise made during an emotional experience in a past life. We are just passing through this lifetime. Our souls don't have an end. We keep going back to the spirit world only to be reborn into another life. I believe that our bodies are our physical vessels and that when we pass on to the other side, we go to a higher dimension. In the higher dimension, there is no time, so to speak, and your soul can come and go as it chooses, to be reborn when it wants. For further understanding of this idea, I suggest Tom Schroeder's book, *Old Soul: the Scientific Evidence for Past Lives*, in which a number of young children speak of previous lives and provide accurate details about them.

Accessing my past lives and understanding the connections I have had with others has helped me heal in so many ways. I am better able to understand the purpose and meaning of my life. Throughout this journey, I have learned many valuable lessons. I am still learning. I sincerely hope that my personal experiences will help others find answers as they explore their own lives, past and present.

References

Brennan, Barbara Ann. *Light Emerging: The Journey of Personal Healing.* New York: Bantam Books, 1993.

Gaudreau, Tick. *Spirit Rescue: A Dowser's Ghostly Encounter.* Bloomington, IN: iUniverse, 2006.

Gee, Judee. *Intuition: Awakening Your Inner Guide.* York Beach, ME: Red Wheel Weiser, 1999.

Holland, John. *Power of the Soul, Inside Wisdom for an Outside World.* Carlsbad, CA: Hay House, 2007.

Newton, Michael. *Destiny of Souls: New Case Studies of Life Between Lives.* 2nd ed. St. Paul, MN: Llewellyn Publications, 2000.

Pitkin, David. *Ghosts of the Northeast.* Chestertown, NY: Aurora Publications, 2002.

Pitkin, David. *Haunted Saratoga County.* Chestertown, NY: Aurora Publications, 2005.

Schroeder, Tom. *Old Souls: The Scientific Evidence for Past Lives.* New York: Simon & Schuster, 1999.

Van Praagh, James. *Reaching to Heaven: A Spiritual Journey Through Life and Death.* New York: Dutton, 1999.

Weiss, Brian, M.D. *Mirrors of Time: Using Regression for Physical, Emotional, and Spiritual_Healing.* Carlsbad, CA: Hay House, 2002.